Old CLYDEBANK

by

Sheila Struthers

Dumbarton Road in 1904. The gap site next to the church was later occupied by the library, which opened in 1913.

First Published in the United Kingdom, 1994
By Richard Stenlake, Ochiltree Sawmill, The Lade, Ochiltree, Ayrshire KA18 2NX
Telephone: 01290 700266

ISBN 1-872074-40-5

To the memory of my gran and great-aunt Mrs. Mary White
and Mrs. Marion McKenzie (nees Fraser)
who died earlier this year.

Dalmuir, looking east along Dumbarton Road.

FOREWORD

Although the area surrounding today's Clydebank has been inhabited since prehistoric times, witnessed the construction of the nearby Antonine wall whilst under Roman occupation and suffered Viking raids, the story of Clydebank itself is a much more recent one.

Clydebank had its beginnings when J. & G. Thomson's Clyde Bank Shipyard were forced to move downstream because the Clyde Navigation Trust compulsorily purchased their Govan yard to build a new dock. In 1871, they acquired a new site between the villages of Yoker and Dalmuir, on farmland which included the tiny village Barns O' Clyde, opposite the mouth of the River Cart. "Tamson's Toon" expanded as housing and other facilities for the shipyard workers were built.

Between 1884 and 1885, the completion of the Singer Manufacturing Co.'s gigantic new factory brought another influx of workers to an already rapidly expanding population.

In 1886, despite strong opposition, the area, comprising of Dalmuir, Clydebank and parts of Kilbowie and Yoker, became a Police Burgh. James Rodger Thomson of shipyard fame, one of the chief exponents of this radical change to the district's administrative structure, was elected Provost at the first meeting of the newly elected Burgh Commissioners. At the same meeting, although one suggestion put forward was Kilbowie, it was decided to name the new burgh Clydebank.

Despite full order books, Thomsons got into financial difficulties and eventually lost control of the business. John Brown & Co., a Sheffield steel manufacturer, acquired the shipyard in 1899. This provided a market for their own products and allowed them to take full advantage of the abundance of naval work which was available at this time.

Napier Shank's & Bell were another firm of Govan shipbuilders who, like Thomson's, had to move downstream to make way for the Clyde Navigation Trust's Princes Dock. Their workforce made a significant contribution to the area's mushrooming population and tenements sprung up along the Yoker end of Glasgow Road as a result.

In 1898, the firm were evicted again for the same reason; the Trust required the land for a vast new mineral dock and the shipbuilders had to move. This photograph was taken two or three years after the Rothesay Dock's official opening, which was in 1907.

The tenement on the left is Clydebank Terrace (Thomson's Building), built by J. & G. Thomson at the same time as they established the shipyard. This 1910 picture shows John Brown & Co. workers leaving the yard by the main gate.

To the right of the picture are some rather grand public toilets.

"The Red House", at the corner of Canal Street, sold industrial clothing and uniforms to shipyard workers and sailors. The foremen at John Brown's wore bowler hats, which earned them the nickname "Hat-men".

The building on the right was Simione's Cafe which, according to several people, sold the best "'Tali" ice-cream in town.

Although, during the early days, Brown's profitability was dependent on securing naval contracts, the glamorous transatlantic liners are what seem to fascinate most people.

The Lusitania, commissioned by Cunard as a sister ship for the Newcastle built Mauretania, was launched in 1906. Second and third class facilities, although lacking the over the top extravagance of first class, were also finished to an extremely high standard.

When war broke out, the Lusitania, unlike many merchant ships, was not requisitioned but continued to operate on the Liverpool-New York passenger run. Nevertheless, controversy surrounds the extent of Admiralty involvement with the finance, fitting out and wartime operation of the ship.

In 1915, the Lusitania was heading for Liverpool when she was sunk off the coast of Ireland, by a German U-boat. This apparently deliberate act of aggression, against a merchant ship carrying civilians (many of whom were Americans), outraged Britain and America. The public outcry of U.S. citizens was such that it was one of the main factors which eventually brought America into the war.

In 1930, the whole country was suffering the effects of the depression; the order books of John Brown's were empty and closure looked inevitable ... It was under these circumstances that the vital order for the massive Cunard passenger liner no. 534 was won.

However, only a year later, Cunard themselves got into financial difficulties and all work, with the exception of essential maintenance, was brought to a standstill for two and a half years.

When work on the ship resumed, with the help of a government subsidy following the merger of Cunard with the White Star Line in 1934, Clydebank heaved a communal sigh of relief.

This year marks the 60th anniversary of her launch, which was on the 26th of September 1934.

The photograph shows the great liner's playroom – far too good for kids if you ask me … and full of what are now highly collectable and very expensive antique toys!

This row of houses (Atlas Street), and another behind it which faces into Glasgow Road, are known as the Atlas Cottages and were built to house the foremen of John Brown & Co. Just out of the picture, to the left, stands the old Caledonian Railway Station.

Until recently this elaborate Victorian building was in a sad state of disrepair, but is now being converted into part of a new development of flats called Cunard Court. Just in case anyone has always fancied living in the old Caley station – Sorry ... they're all sold.

1918 – when the grocer formed individual pats from a huge slab of butter, cut cheese with a wire from the whole and carefully weighed and packaged dry goods to order.

This is Whitecrook Co-op (no.4 branch) in Cochno Street. The building, erected in 1907, is still there today; what was the Co-op transport office is next door and the old dairy and stabling block are off the yard behind.

Personal service from individual shopkeepers is sadly missed today.
This picture of Glasgow Road, looking west, dates from the 1940s......

......and in 1958, this area was still the town's main shopping centre.
The City Bakeries, scene of many a wedding reception, is on the right.

Kilbowie Road, from The Cross, circa 1913. A. Booth's Clydebank Bar is obscured by the tram; T.F. Ross's public house is just out of the picture to the right.

This much busier photograph was taken about 30 years later.

Kilbowie Road, circa 1910. The building on the left, Singer Terrace, was built by Singer to provide accommodation for 60 of the factory's foremen, fire-men and watchmen. Although this was the only worker's accommodation built by the company itself, speculative property developers were quick to meet the demand and tenements appeared on Kilbowie Road and the streets leading off it.

The wooden bascule canal bridge, after long and tortured negotiations between Clydebank Burgh and Glasgow Corporation over who should pay for what, was eventually replaced by this metal swingbridge, to allow the latter's tram system to extend along Kilbowie Road.

The canal bridge at Dalmuir, caused similar problems and was also the subject of much disagreement.

This photograph, showing Singer Terrace and Hope Terrace, should bring back plenty of memories; the Palace picture house, the Kilbowie Bar and the Rossdhu Bar are all on the sunny side of Kilbowie Road.

This aerial view gives an idea of the vast scale of the Singer Factory. The American company came to Glasgow in 1856 in a successful attempt to break into the European market. The Scottish branch of the company expanded in piecemeal fashion as demand for sewing machines continued to increase, but it became clear that efficiency would be greatly increased if all the various operations could be carried out on one site.

Work began on the Kilbowie factory in 1882. Despite excellent road, rail, canal and river links, this was the company's second choice of sites. The factory was built by Robert McAlpine & Co., who at the time were a little known firm. Robert McAlpine went on to become a very successful and somewhat controversial figure in Clydebank.

The enormous capital investment paid off for the company and business flourished. In 1906, an additional building was built and extra storeys were added to the existing ones. Still more space was required and the grounds of the factory were extended northwards across the North British Railway line. Singer Station replaced Kilbowie Station when the railway company rebuilt the line.

Despite the Clydebank factory switching most of its production to the manufacture of munitions for the duration of the war, and although Singer's lost almost half its market and had to forfeit all its Russian capital investment following the 1917 revolution, output was almost back to 1913 figures by the 1920s.

Although the depression years of the 30s were difficult times for all, the Clydebank factory was not as badly affected as many other local employers. During the Second World War, production was again devoted to the war effort. Despite suffering damage, the factory survived the terrible nights of the Blitz and by 1945 business was booming.

However Singer management, lulled into a false sense of security, failed to move with the times. It was the workers of Clydebank who were to pay the price for their lack of foresight and failure to invest in new plant and new ideas.

1946 saw the start of a slow decline. Singer's, although it still dominated the industrial sewing machine market, found itself facing competition from modern factories producing domestic machines in Europe and Japan. In the 1960s the company invested in one new building, with state of the art equipment, to compete in the European and American domestic sewing machine markets, but the industrial sewing machine division, still sadly in need of modernisation, was ignored. That well kent landmark, the Singer Clock, was demolished to make way for this new building.

In the 1970s the European and American markets went into decline. Despite a hard fought battle by union representatives, the factory finally closed in 1980.

DO YOU KNOW
THAT . . . . LITTLE
SINGER MOTOR?

One screw attaches it to your machine

Cuts out all fatigue!
Makes sewing a pleasure!
Better work done in half the time!

And then—after dark, that Little

SINGERLIGHT

—by showing the stitching more clearly—prevents eyestrain and saves time and annoyance when threading the needle

Any Singer Shop or Singer Salesman will tell you all about them

Singer, in common with other major employers, supported and encouraged a variety of leisure activities for its workers.

In 1928 there were also: a Ladies' Athletic Association, Football Association, Boys' Recreation Association, Operatic Society, Chess and Draughts Club, Hockey Club, Pipe Band, Badminton Club, Camera Club, The Singer Players (amateur dramatics), Tennis Club, Golf Association, Orchestral Society, Horticultural Society, Whist Club … and a rather dubious sounding Physical Culture Club (keep fit).

It's a wonder that anyone ever got any work done!

Opposite Singer Station and "down a wee tunnel" was the New Kinema picture house. Above the Co-op, Mitchell's the dentist. The billiard hall in the middle of the block was used as an air raid shelter during the war. Despite, or maybe because of, the fear that the air raid sirens must have caused and the horror of 13th and 14th of March 1941 when Clydebank was devastated by relentless bombing, it's the amusing stories which are told and retold:

One woman sorely tried the patience of the other inhabitants of her close. As they sheltered together, on the mild spring night of the 13th, enduring the terrifying sounds of the bombs setting Clydebank ablaze…… her main concern was that her son should periodically run upstairs to check that the fire was "still in!"

Further up Kilbowie Road, circa 1912. Off to the right is Montrose Street, one of the original streets of the district, which was there long before any of the tenements on the Hill. Further along Montrose Street and past the cemetery, was the "Soor Milk Farm".

A later picture taken from further up Kilbowie Road. Although the first obstacle to the extension of the tramway system up Kilbowie Road was overcome when the old canal bridge was replaced in 1916, it wasn't until 1924 that old Paisley district trams were converted into single deckers, which could fit under the low railway bridges, and the system was extended as far as Singer Station. By the following year trams were running all the way to Duntocher. The fare on the "Wee Trams", from the foot of Kilbowie Road to Roman Road Duntocher, was $^{1}/_{2}$d.

Radnor Park was at one time a separate community, surrounded by fields and with uninterrupted views to the south and west. In the 1880s, more and more of the surrounding land was bought up and developed. This photograph shows one of the original streets, Granville Street.

Radnor Park suffered especially badly during the Blitz:
During a lull in the bombing, on the night of the 14th, one young woman made a mad dash from the relative safety of the air-raid shelter, back to the remains of her Radnor Street home. It was the eve of her wedding and she was not going to abandon her wedding dress because of a few bombs! However the tattered dress, so daringly rescued, soon lay forgotten as she devoted the rest of the night to battling against fires and helping the injured. The following day, despite the horrific aftermath, the couple were married. The bride wore a "cinderella" style wedding dress and two smoke-stained black eyes.

Second Avenue looking East, Clydebank.

Although many Clydebank employees resided in Radnor Park, the area did not become a part of the Burgh until 1906.

The "Holy City", so-called because its terraces of flat roofs were reminiscent of postcard views of Jerusalem, was built by Robert McAlpine. Work began shortly before Radnor Park became a part of Clydebank Burgh and as a result the buildings were not subject to the strict building regulations which would have applied had the development been within the Burgh boundary. In 1905, when the oldest of the houses were only a year old, some tenants were withholding rent in protest at their landlords' failure to carry out essential repairs – To my mind, building flat roofed houses on a wet and windy West of Scotland hillside was asking for trouble!

During the Blitz, Second Avenue took a direct hit which tore the whole front off one of the buildings, resulting in the deaths of 80 people.

This photograph shows “Mary with the Brown’s Church Choir” – which of the two crosses marks Mary, I don’t know. The man sitting proudly between the trophies is Broughton Chatford, choirmaster from 1905-1955.

The Radnor Park Parish Church was better known as Brown’s Church, after its founder the Rev. Orr Brown. The original church building, which was opened in 1895, suffered a series of disasters: It went on fire in 1909 and although badly damaged was restored. It was again damaged by fire during the Blitz and again restored. Fire struck for the third time during the January storm of 1968 and this time the damage was so great that the building had to be demolished.

A new church was built in 1970 …… and in 1973 was set on fire by vandals.

One way in which the Town Council tried to overcome shortages of skilled labour and building materials during the inter-war years was to experiment with new materials and methods of construction. "The Bungalows" were constructed to a design based on two experimental houses built by Thomas Rae, superintendent of Clydebank and District Water Trust, beside the Cochno filter plant. They had solid concrete walls which were made by allowing the concrete to set between wooden shutters. The shutters were then used to form joists for the roofs.

These houses in Bell Street are another example of 1920s non-traditional house construction, their frames and walls being made of steel. Atholl Steel Houses Ltd. were a subsidiary of Beardmore's. Demand for these houses provided much-needed work for the company's locomotive works, which were idle due to lack of orders at the time.

In Edwardian times, many people's social life revolved around the churches and other religious organisations.

The message on the back of this postcard reads:
"Dear Mother,
This was taken in front of the late Lord Overtoun's house. Had a splendid day in the grounds and then had tea in Dumbarton. Puzzle, find yours truly.
from Alfred"

The Union Church and St. James Church, were the oldest in Clydebank, established in 1877 and 1876 respectively.

Between Dalmuir and Yoker, by the canal on the north side of Dumbarton Road, stood a house called Standalane. The original Union Church, which was demolished in 1892 to make way for the North British Railway, was built on this site. This church, its replacement, was built directly across the road and opened in 1894. Sadly "the Cathedral of Clydebank", as this fine building was affectionately nick-named, recently had to be demolished following a fire.

The canal, completed in 1790, was already about 120 years old when this picture was taken.

Its main purposes were to facilitate trade links with Europe and to transport heavy goods such as coal, iron ore and limestone, which were increasingly in demand by the emerging industries of the time. Passenger services were also operated and pleasure cruises continued long after faster means of transport, by road and rail, had taken over the main routes.

Dumbarton Road, looking west, circa 1913.

This view, looking north towards "The Hill" with its fine villas, shows Hillview Terrace on the left and Dalmuir School on the right.

This 1903 photograph, looks east along Dumbarton Road, from just across the bridge. The tramway system was extended as far as the canal bridge in 1904.

In 1908, the Dunbartonshire tram system was extended to Dalmuir West ($^{1}/_{4}$ of a mile west of the canal) and hordes of Glaswegians, bound for Balloch and the Bonnie Banks, descended upon Dalmuir every weekend. The fact that as "bona-fide travellers" daytrippers were allowed to purchase alcoholic beverages on a Sunday, made these excursions all the more enjoyable for the tourists and all the more profitable for those providing extortionately priced refreshments in Balloch.

This new bridge, which allowed the trams to run without interruption to Dalmuir West, was not opened until 1915.

In 1900, William Beardmore of the highly successful Parkhead Forge, acquired the Govan shipyard of long established and valued customer Robert Napier & Sons (at this time many steel manufacturers were securing outlets for their products in similar ways). However, Beardmore, a flamboyant character, thought big, and the yard he built at Dalmuir was on a different scale altogether.

This photograph, looks across Dalmuir Station towards Beardmore's Naval Construction works. It was taken in 1905, a year before the yard's official opening, when the battleship Agamemnon was launched.

The "gap" in the otherwise rather handsome semi-circular terrace which was known as "The Crescent", was due to a withdrawal of finance following the collapse of the City of Glasgow Bank in 1878.

Most of the tenements in Dalmuir were built by Beardmore to house his workforce. The Beardmore Building, on the left, was built in 1906 to house some of the work's foremen. Each house had two rooms, a kitchen and a bathroom! – albeit with cold water only. A more standard design, for the majority of the workforce, had one room, a kitchen, and … an inside w.c.

During the First World War, Beardmore's was continually expanding, as what had started as a shipyard and engine works, diversified to produce submarines, artillery, tanks, planes and airships (the aviation department was across the river at Inchinnan).

Accommodation for the greatly increased workforce became a problem and a second phase of tenement building was begun. Wartime shortages of material meant that these buildings, on the south side of Dumbarton Road (to the left of this 30s picture), were finished with flat roofs.

After the war, much of the new plant which had been acquired during the war years was converted to locomotive manufacture, the shipyard was extended and the company's aviation department continued its innovative work.

However, by the beginning of the 1920s it was clear that the post-war boom was not to last. The unforeseen downturn in trade meant that massive running costs drained the company's already stretched financial reserves. The closure of the yard was announced in September 1930.

The last order completed by the aviation department, the passenger car for the Bennie Rail-Plane, was typical of the Beardmore's commitment to new and adventurous ideas. George Bennie visualised his monorail system linking the country's major cities. There was plenty of interest, including the suggestion that the rail-plane be used at the 1938 Empire Exhibition, but sadly this novel system was only ever put into operation on this 426 yard length of experimental track at Milngavie.

Dumbarton Road circa 1919. The shop at the corner of Trafalgar Street, was called Bonanza's and owned by the Muir family. The millinery department window was a source of great amusement to the younger members of the families in the tenement opposite – I don't expect that the women primping and posing in front of the mirror, as they tried on different styles, knew that they had such an appreciative audience!

Dalmuir Park, opened in 1906 with much pomp and ceremony, was the Burgh's first park. Visible among the trees, is Dalmuir House which, with 12½ acres of surrounding ground, became a part of the park in 1908. It was demolished in the 1920s.

Of all the many events which the park has hosted over the decades, the annual "Illuminations", during which the park was all aglow with brightly coloured decorations, are what people seem to recall with most fondness. The Illuminations were begun in 1945 as part of the V.E. Day celebrations and continued until the 1960s.

Perhaps due to lack of funding, organised activities in the park seem to be almost a thing of the past.

"If Radio Clyde can organise concerts in Glasgow's Kelvingrove Park, you'd think they could manage something on their own doorstep," was one point made to me.

The children's playground was originally close to Duntocher Road, down by the railway line. When Dunswin Court and Overtoun Court were built, the high flats overshadowed the area and the playground was moved to its present site.

Salvation Army Band open-air meetings were a regular Sunday morning occurrence, which, despite the sad loss of musicians, instruments, uniforms and music, even the devastation of the Blitz was not allowed to interrupt.

The Bandmaster here is James Borthwick, who held the position between 1915 and 1961, with the exception of the 1st World War years.

James Borthwick (far left) also provided the young people's band with help and advice.

He died, in 1975, at the grand old age of 83. The great sadness of the event was tempered by the fitting manner of his death; he collapsed immediately after having conducted the massed brass bands of Hamilton, Clydebank and Bo'n-ess, in his favourite hymn "Wondrous Cross".

It was said, at the time, that the last line of this hymn – "Love so amazing, so divine, demands my soul, my life, my all" – was an apt tribute to this popular man.

Local rivals:

Left to right: Back row: J. McGorm, S. Hynds, J. Lang, T. McLaughlan, A. McFarlane (capt.), A. McBride.

Front row: W. Baggley, J. Stevenson, F. Forsyth, H. Smillie, G. Tuck.

While questioning a veteran fan on the local history of the game, I was warned – "for God's sake get the footie facts right or you'll be getting letters forever more!"

the teams of 1936

Left to right. Back row: W. McLean, W. Milne, H. Scott, A. Fulton, W. Colvin, S. Boyd (capt.)

Front row: T. Ferguson, A. Howie, J. Weir, W. Forbes, R. Wilson.

Clydebank Juniors once met Yoker Athletic in the final of the County Cup. Yoker won. However, their triumph was short-lived. When it came to light that Yoker had played a man whose club had been suspended due to an unpaid debt, a replay was ordered.

It was probably just as well that Yoker won the replay – the unfortunate player's share of the debt was only fourpence halfpenny!

Yoker grew up around both sides of the Yoker Burn, which used to be the boundary between Renfrewshire and Dunbartonshire and today divides Glasgow from Clydebank. It expanded to become a proper village after Harvey's Distillery was established around 1740. There has been a ford here and later a ferry, since ancient times.

This wonderfully atmospheric picture shows the first steam ferry, which came into service in 1868, at Renfrew. Looking across to Yoker – Clydebank House is on the left and the Ferry House is on the right with Clydebank Cottage next to it.

Still at Renfrew, circa 1911, looking across the river towards a much changed Yoker. The power station, just visible on the far left, was built in 1905.

This second ferry, which was driven by two chains, replaced the original single chain ferry in 1897.

The third steam ferry, which came into service in 1912, at Renfrew.

The much larger, fourth and last steam ferry operated from 1935 until 1952, when a diesel ferry was put into operation.

This photograph is taken at Yoker.

It seems that this puss has been on the prowl along the canal banks! Walks along the towpaths were popular with everyone, but especially so with couples in search of a romantic setting for their courting.